Insects

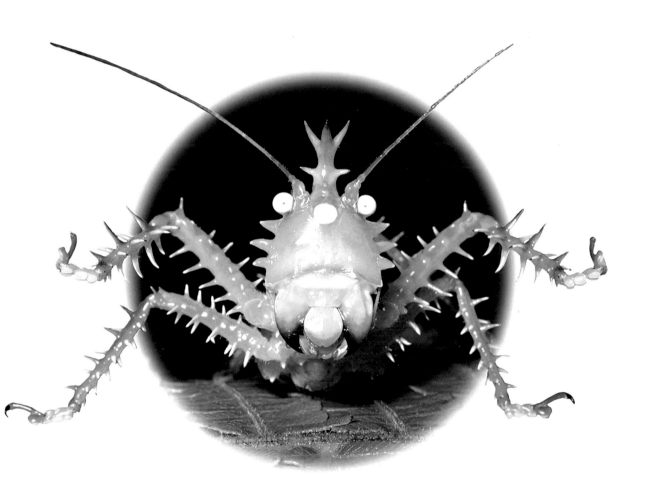

KINGFISHER

Published in 2010 by Kingfisher
This edition published in 2013 by Kingfisher
an imprint of Macmillan Children's Books
a division of Macmillan Publishers Limited
20 New Wharf Road
London N1 9RR
Basingstoke and Oxford
Associated companies throughout the world
www.panmacmillan.com

ISBN 978-0-7534-3725-4

First published as *Kingfisher Young Knowledge: Insects* in 2006
Additional material produced for Macmillan Children's Books by Discovery Books Ltd

Copyright © Macmillan Children's Books 2010

1 3 5 7 9 8 6 4 2
1SPL/0713/WKT/UTD/128MA

A CIP catalogue record for this book is available from the British Library.

Printed in China

Note to readers: the website addresses listed in this book are correct at
the time of going to print. However, due to the ever-changing nature
of the internet, website addresses and content can change. Websites
can contain links that are unsuitable for children. The publisher cannot
be held responsible for changes in website addresses or content, or
for information obtained through a third party. We strongly advise
that internet searches should be supervised by an adult.

Acknowledgements
The publishers would like to thank the following for permission to reproduce their material. Every care has been taken
to trace copyright holders. However, if there have been unintentional omissions or failure to trace copyright holders,
we apologize and will, if informed, endeavour to make corrections in any future edition.
b = bottom, *c* = centre, *l* = left, *t* = top, *r* = right

Cover Shutterstock/Subbotina Anna; Shutterstock/Butterfly Hunter; Shutterstock/Florian Andronache; Shutterstock/Marco Uliana; *pages* 1 Frank Lane Picture Agency
(FLPA)/Michael & Patricia Fogden; 2-3 Nature Picture Library (Naturepl)/Ingo Arndt; 4–5 Corbis/Michael & Patricia Fogden; 6-7 FLPA/Minden; 7*tr* FLPA/Panda Photo;
7*br* Getty Dorling Kindersley; 8*l* FLPA/Foto Natura; 8–9 FLAP/Roger Wilmshurst; 9*r* FLPA/B. Borrell Casals; 10*b* Ardea/Pascal Goetgheluck; 10–11 FLPA/Minden;
11*tr* Ardea/Steve Hopkin; 12 FLPA/Minden; 12-13 Naturepl/Ingo Arndt; 13*tr* Natural History Picture Agency (NHPA)/ Stephen Dalton; 14*cr* NHPA/James Carmichael;
14*cl* FLPA/Foto Natura; 14*bl* Naturepl/Duncan McEwan; 15 Photolibrary.com; 16 NHPA/Paal Hermansen; 17*t* Ardea/Steve Hopkin; 17*b* FLPA/Minden;
18 Photolibary.com; 19*t* Photolibrary.com; 19*b* FLPA/Derek Middleton; 20*bl* Naturepl/Premaphotos; 21*tr* FLPA/Richard Becker; 21*b* FLPA/Foto Natura; 22*lc* Science
Photo Library (SPL)/Susumu Nishinaga; 22*bl* Naturepl/Warwick Sloss; 23*t* Ardea/Steve Hopkin; 23*cl* SPL/Nuridsany & Perennou; 23*cr* SPL/Susumu Nishinaga;
23*br* Naturepl/Ross Hoddinott; 24-25 Naturepl/Premaphotos; 24*b* FLPA/Foto Natura; 25*br* Ardea/John Mason; 26 Corbis/Anthony Bannister; 26*bl* FLPA/Foto Natura;
27*b* Naturepl/Martin Dohrn; 28*cl* Alamy; 28*br* Photolibrary.com; 29 Naturepl/Michael Durham; 29*b* Getty NGS; 30 Corbis/Anthony Bannister; 31*t* NHPA/George
Bernard; 31*b* FLPA/Foto Natura; 32 FLPA/Minden 33*tr* FLPA/Derek Middleton; 33*b* FLPA/Minden; 34-35 Photolibrary.com; 34*b* Photolibrary.com; 35*tr* Photolibrary.com;
36 Photolibrary.com; 37*t* Naturepl/Martin Dohrn; Corbis/Anthony Bannister; 38 Alamy/Peter Arnold Inc.; 39*t* Alamy/Robert Pickett; 39*b* Alamy/Maximilian Weinzierl;
48*t* Shutterstock Images/Yaroslav; 48*b* Shutterstock Images/Christian Musat; 49*t* Shutterstock Images/Jamie Wilson; 49*c* Shutterstock Images/Le Do; 52*t* Shutterstock
Images/Yellowj; 52*b* Shutterstock Images/M Dykstra; 53*t* Shutterstock Images/Dark Raptor; 53*b* Shutterstock Images/Javarman; 56*t* Shutterstock Images/Zvenis

Commissioned photography on pages 42–47 by Andy Crawford
Thank you to models Alex Bandy, Alastair Carter, Tyler Gunning and Lauren Signist

Insects

Barbara Taylor

KINGFISHER

Contents

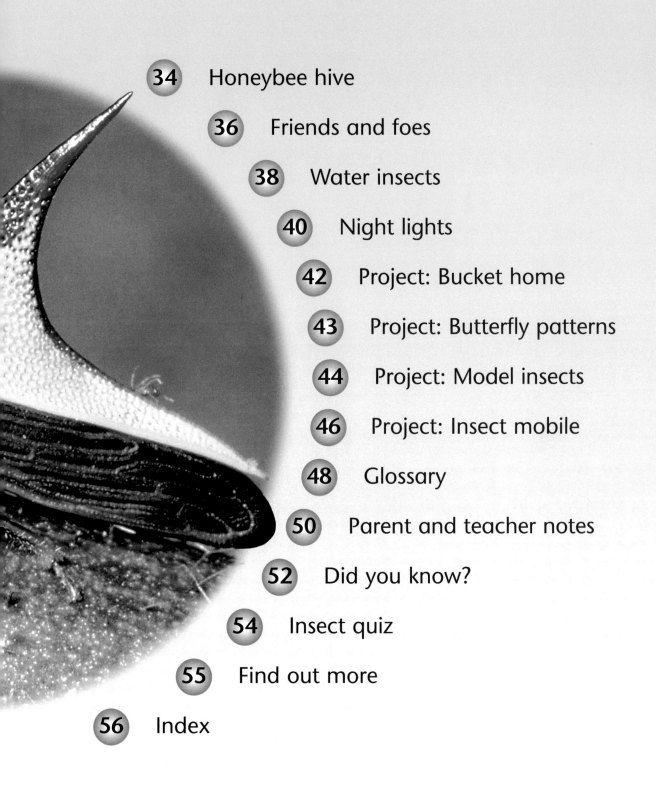

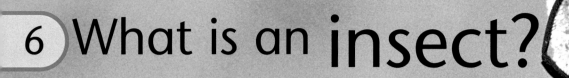

What is an insect?

An insect is a small animal with six legs and three parts to its body. A hard outer skeleton covers and protects an insect's body like a suit of armour.

dragonfly

On the wing

Most insects have one or two pairs of wings. Their wings are thin flaps that are made from the outer body covering. They are joined to the middle part of an insect's body, which is called the thorax.

Early insects

The first insects lived on Earth over 400 million years ago, long before people were around. This insect was trapped in the sticky sap oozing from a tree and preserved for millions of years.

Not an insect!

Spiders, such as this house spider, are not insects. Spiders have eight legs and only two parts to their body. The head and thorax are joined together. They do not have wings either.

All kinds of insects

There are millions of different kinds of insects, which are divided into groups such as beetles, butterflies and moths, bees, wasps, flies and bugs.

Wasps

Wasps belong to a group of insects that also includes bees and ants. A wasp has a narrow 'waist' and folds its wings along the sides of its body.

Flies

A fly has only one pair of wings,
yet it can fly very well.
The fly group includes
mosquitoes, and
bluebottles like this.

Butterflies

Butterflies and moths have wings
covered in tiny scales, which overlap
like tiles on a roof. Butterflies, such
as this swallowtail, are usually
brightly coloured and fly by day.

Big and small insects

Most insects are small beasts – even the biggest ones could sit on your hand. Their small size means they can live in small spaces and do not need much food.

Tiny fleas

Fleas live among the fur of mammals or the feathers of birds. They have claws to cling on tight, and long legs to jump from one animal to another.

Nasty nits

Head lice thrive in the warmth of human hair, sucking blood from our skin. Female head lice glue their eggs on to the hair. These are known as nits.

Giant weta

Wetas are giant crickets that live in New Zealand. They probably grew into huge insects because there were no large mammal predators, or hunters, to eat them.

Insect athletes

Some insects are like human athletes. They are champion sprinters, high jumpers or weightlifters. Insects use their athletic powers to find food or mates, or just to stay alive.

Weightlifting
One of these male rhinoceros beetles has managed to lift the other right off the ground! He wins the chance to mate with the females.

High jump

Insects that are good at the high jump, such as this leafhopper, usually have long back legs powered by strong muscles in the thorax.

Sprinting

Long legs help insects to take big strides and sprint (move fast). The legs of this tiger beetle are much longer than its body. At any time, three of its six legs usually touch the ground.

Wonder wings

Insects were the first animals to fly. Flying helps insects to find food or mates and to escape danger, but it does use up a lot of energy.

Long journeys

Monarch butterflies fly thousands of kilometres every year to escape the cold winters in Canada. These long journeys are called migration.

Wing covers

Beetles, such as this ladybird, have two pairs of wings. When a beetle lands, its hard front wings cover and protect the delicate flying wings.

Strong wings

A network of veins in
an insect's wings makes
them strong and flexible.
You can see the veins
very clearly on this
cicada's wings.

Clever colours

Dull colours help insects to hide from predators. Bright colours or patterns warn predators to stay away because an insect is poisonous or harmful.

Warning colours

The bright red spots on this burnet moth are a warning message, which says: 'Don't eat me. I contain deadly poison.'

Fake wasp

The wasp beetle cannot sting and is not dangerous. Predators leave it alone because they think it is a real wasp and might sting them.

Hide and seek

Many insects use camouflage to hide from predators by looking like the plants they live on. This thorn bug even has a pretend thorn on its back!

Fighting back

From sharp jaws to painful stings and chemical weapons, insects have many ways of fighting back when they are attacked by predators.

Ready, aim, fire!
Bombardier beetles spray boiling hot poisons at their enemies. The poisons are mixed up inside the beetles' bodies when danger threatens.

Horrible hiss
If these cockroaches are disturbed, they make a loud, hissing noise by pushing air out of breathing holes in their sides. This startles predators, such as spiders, giving the cockroaches time to escape.

Battling beetle

The devil's coachhorse beetle defends itself by curling its abdomen over its back like a scorpion. At the same time, the beetle gives off a nasty smell, and snaps its jaws together.

Insect senses

An insect's senses of sight, touch, smell and hearing are vital to its survival. These senses are often much better than our own but they work in different ways.

Touch and smell

Insects use their antennae to touch and smell their surroundings. This weevil's antennae have special hairs at the tips to detect smells.

Head fans

Scarab beetles fan out their antennae when they fly to increase their size. This helps the beetles detect any smells.

Eye spy

The big eyes of this fly are made up of thousands of very small eyes. They can see in lots of different directions at once.

Hungry insects

Some insects, such as cockroaches, eat almost anything, but most insects feed on particular kinds of food. Their mouthparts help them to hold and chop up solid food, or suck up liquids.

Spongy mouth

Flies turn their food into a soupy mush, and then use a spongy pad (left) to mop up their meal. They can also taste their food with their feet!

Jagged jaws

Insect predators need sharp, spiky jaws for holding and chopping up their prey. Insects that chew plants have blunter jaws to grind and mash up their food.

Drinking straws

Butterflies and moths feed on liquid food, such as flower nectar or rotting fruit. They suck up their food through a tube, called a proboscis, which works like a straw.

Nibbling plants

All the different parts of plants are eaten by insects. Some plant-eating insects are farmers, growing their own crops and harvesting seeds.

Leaves for lunch

Leaves do not contain much goodness, so insects have to eat a lot of them. Grasshoppers are messy eaters, often tearing the leaves as they feed.

Grow-your-own food

Leafcutter ants chew up pieces of leaves and use them to make a mushy compost. They grow fungi on the compost, so they always have plenty to eat.

Wood for supper

Wood contains even less goodness than leaves, but some insects eat it. Death-watch beetle larvae spend many years eating damp wood before turning into adults like this one.

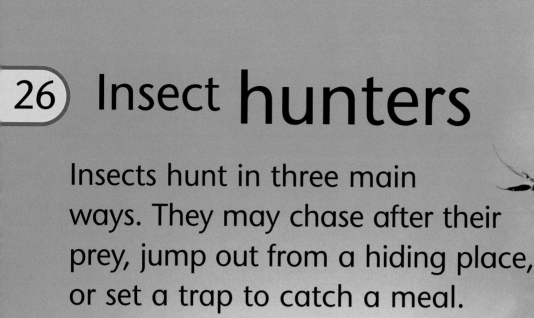

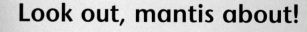

Insect hunters

Insects hunt in three main ways. They may chase after their prey, jump out from a hiding place, or set a trap to catch a meal. Most insects hunt alone, but a few search in groups.

Look out, mantis about!

Many mantids look like leaves. They keep very still, then shoot out their long front legs to grab a passing insect. A mantis has sharp jaws to slice up its prey and scoop out the soft insides.

Soupy snacks

Robber flies catch flying
insects with their long,
hairy legs. Then they turn
the insides of the prey
into a liquid soup and
suck up their meal.

All together now

Army ants from tropical America
hunt in large groups. The ants help
each other to catch and kill prey.
These army ants have caught
a centipede.

Life cycles

Many insects have four stages in their life cycle – egg, larva, pupa and adult. Insect groups that develop like this include beetles, butterflies, moths, flies, fleas, bees and ants.

1 Egg

A female monarch butterfly lays her eggs underneath the leaves of milkweed plants. Within a week, the eggs hatch into stripy caterpillars.

2 Larva

The hungry caterpillar eats and eats and eats. It sheds its skin several times as it grows. This is called moulting.

3 Pupa

When the caterpillar is big enough, it turns into a pupa, or chrysalis. Inside the pupa, the body of the caterpillar changes into the body of a butterfly.

4 Adult

The pupa splits open, and the adult butterfly pulls itself free. It pumps blood into its wings to stretch them out, and waits for its wings to dry. Then it flies away to look for a mate.

Insect eggs

Almost all insects start life as eggs. The eggs are usually laid on or near food, and hidden from predators and bad weather. Very few insects look after their eggs.

Easy meals

Dung beetles shape animal dung into a ball, which they roll to a safe place. The female lays her eggs inside the dung ball so the young have food when they hatch.

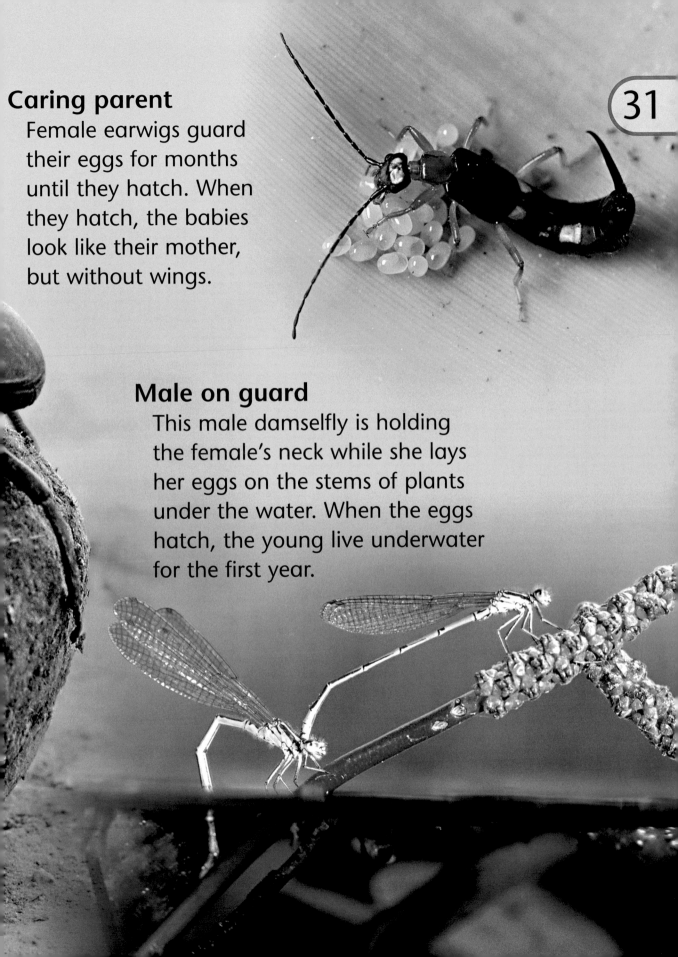

Caring parent

Female earwigs guard their eggs for months until they hatch. When they hatch, the babies look like their mother, but without wings.

Male on guard

This male damselfly is holding the female's neck while she lays her eggs on the stems of plants under the water. When the eggs hatch, the young live underwater for the first year.

Living **together**

Most insects live alone, but a few kinds live and work together in groups. They are called social insects. All ants and termites, and some bees and wasps, are social insects.

Royal ruler
A big, fat queen termite lays all the eggs in a nest. The smaller workers carry her eggs away, and bring food for their queen.

Paper nest

Paper wasps make their nest by chewing up wood and mixing it with their spit to make wasp 'paper'. Inside the nest are lots of tiny boxes, called cells, where young wasps can develop.

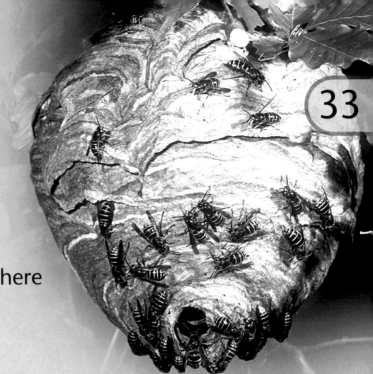

Special sewing

Weaver ants work together as a team to make a nest from leaves glued together with sticky silk. One ant working on its own would not be strong enough to do this.

Honeybee hive

People build artificial nests, called hives, for honeybees. The honeybees make honey from flower nectar mixed with their spit. Bee-keepers take this honey for people to eat.

Wax city

Honeybees use wax made in their bodies to build rows of six-sided boxes, called cells. These cells fit closely together to make a thin sheet called a honeycomb.

Queen bee

The big bee in the middle of this picture is a queen honeybee. She lays all the eggs in a honeybee hive.

Bee-keeper

Bee-keepers lift the honeycombs out to check on the honey and the baby bees inside. They wear special clothes to protect them from bee stings.

Friends and foes

Many insects are our friends because they help flower seeds develop, and are an important link in food chains. Some insects cause problems because they eat crops or carry diseases.

Pollen carriers

Many flowers rely on insects to carry a yellow dust, called pollen, to other flowers of the same kind. Pollen has to join with the eggs inside flowers before seeds can develop.

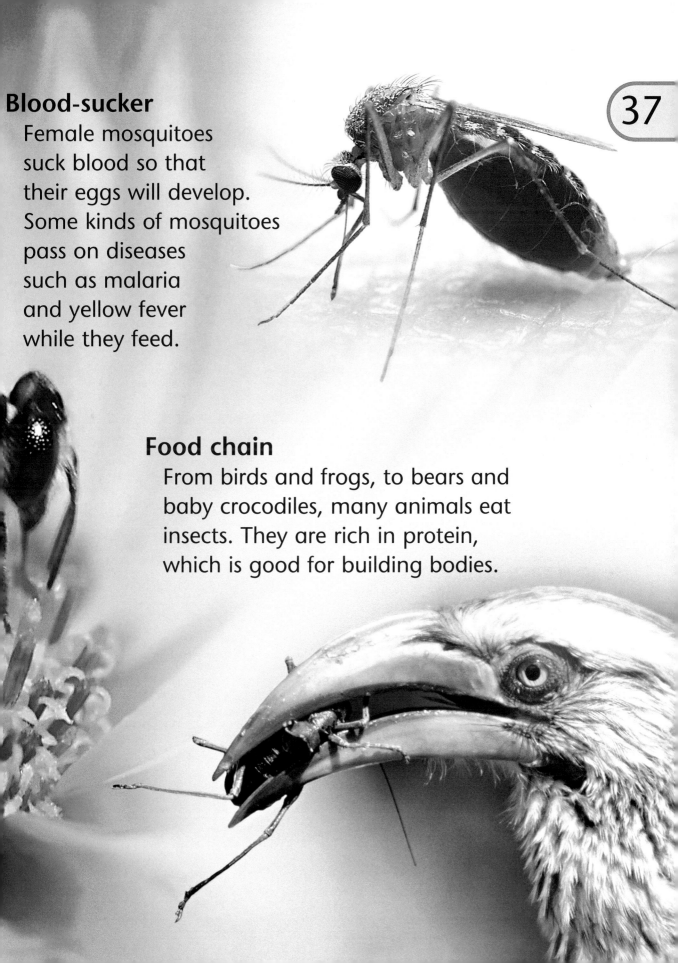

Blood-sucker

Female mosquitoes
suck blood so that
their eggs will develop.
Some kinds of mosquitoes
pass on diseases
such as malaria
and yellow fever
while they feed.

Food chain

From birds and frogs, to bears and
baby crocodiles, many animals eat
insects. They are rich in protein,
which is good for building bodies.

Water insects

Many insects live in fresh water, where there is plenty of food and protection from predators. Some skate over the surface, some swim, while others lurk on the bottom.

Spare air

Great diving beetles collect air from the surface of the water. They store the air under their wing covers, so they can breathe while they are underwater.

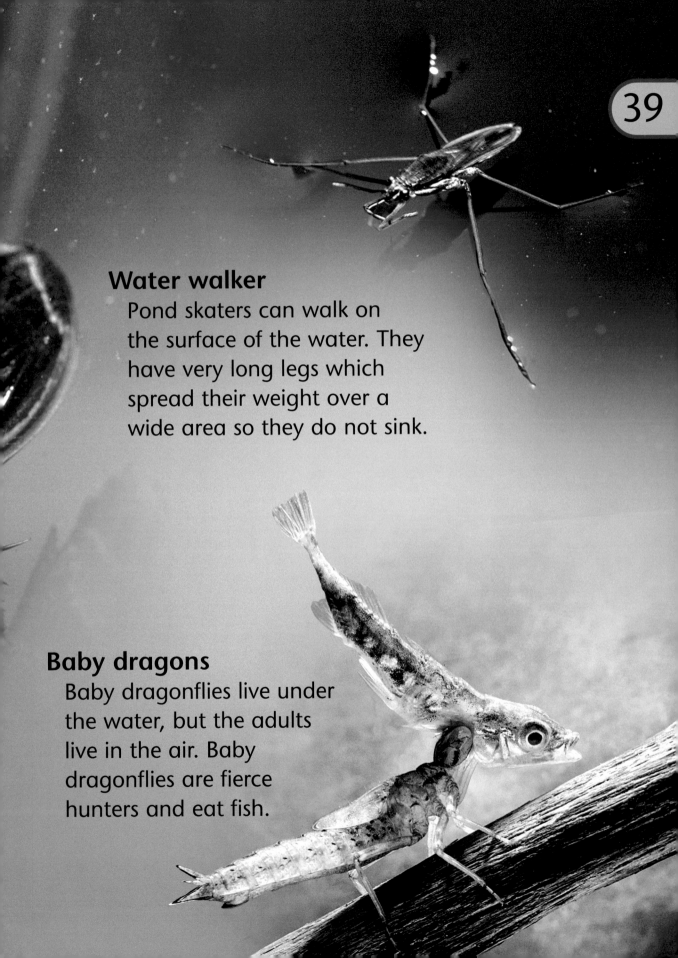

Water walker

Pond skaters can walk on
the surface of the water. They
have very long legs which
spread their weight over a
wide area so they do not sink.

Baby dragons

Baby dragonflies live under
the water, but the adults
live in the air. Baby
dragonflies are fierce
hunters and eat fish.

Night lights

Insects glow in the dark to attract a mate or prey, warn their friends of danger, or tell predators that they taste bad.

Come and get me

Fireflies and glow-worms are beetles that come out at night. Some glow all the time, while others flash their lights on and off in a particular pattern. These light signals are used to attract a mate.

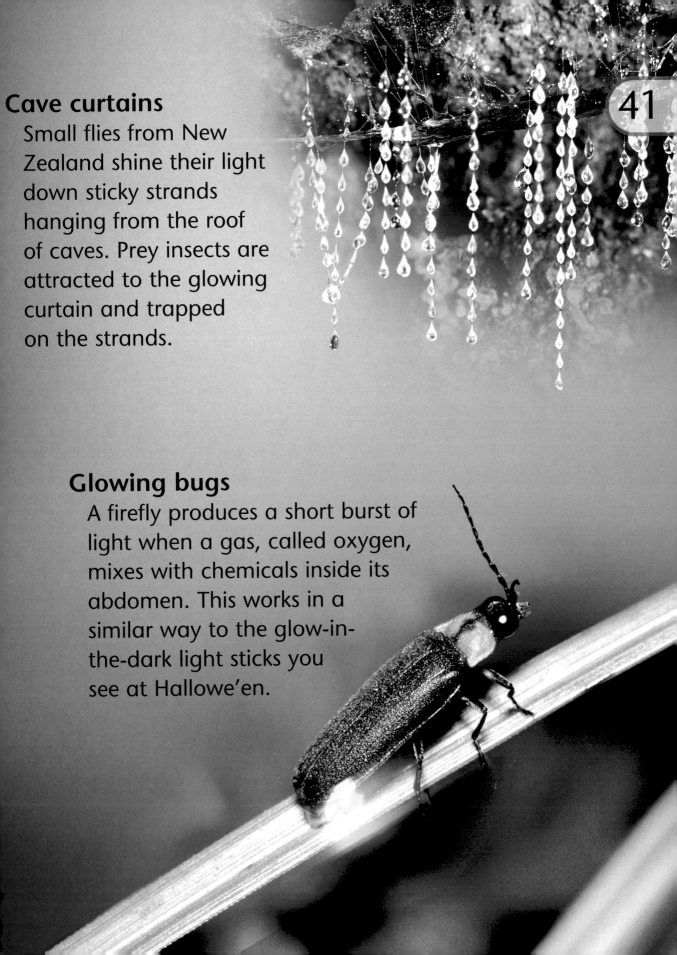

Cave curtains

Small flies from New Zealand shine their light down sticky strands hanging from the roof of caves. Prey insects are attracted to the glowing curtain and trapped on the strands.

Glowing bugs

A firefly produces a short burst of light when a gas, called oxygen, mixes with chemicals inside its abdomen. This works in a similar way to the glow-in-the-dark light sticks you see at Hallowe'en.

Bucket home

Bug sleepover

Make a home for the bugs that live near you. Draw pictures of the bugs that crawl inside, and write down their names.

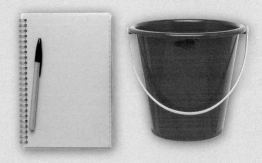

1

You will need
- Plastic bucket
- Pen and notepad
- Stones, leaves and grass

Find a damp, shady place near your home. Turn the bucket upside down and balance it on a pile of stones, leaves and grass. Leave it overnight and see if any creatures crawl inside.

When you have finished, remember to let the animals go.

Butterfly patterns

Paint a butterfly

The patterns on one wing of a butterfly are the same as the other side. Paint your own butterfly with matching sides.

You will need
- Card
- Pencil
- Scissors
- Paint
- Paintbrush
- Pipecleaners

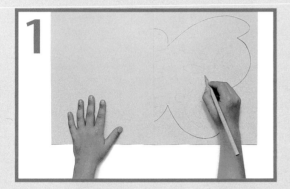

1 Fold the card in half, then open it out flat. Use the pencil to draw the outline of half a butterfly on one side of the fold.

2 Fold the card in half so you can still see your pencil outline. Then carefully cut out the butterfly shape.

Open the card to see the whole butterfly, and use pipecleaners for its antennae.

3 Open out the card and paint one side with thick paint. Then fold your butterfly in half again and press down hard.

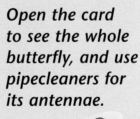

Model insects

Make a ladybird

Use papier mâché to make a model of a giant ladybird. Paint the model red and black, so it looks just like a real ladybird. A ladybird's bright colours warn predators that it is poisonous and tastes bad.

You will need
- Balloon
- Petroleum jelly
- Paintbrush
- Newspaper
- Wallpaper paste
- Scissors
- Paints
- Pipecleaners
- Glue or sticky tape

Ask an adult to help you blow up a balloon. Spread a thick layer of petroleum jelly all over the balloon, then wash your hands.

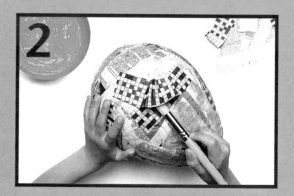

Cover the whole balloon with strips of newspaper. Brush wallpaper paste over the paper and repeat about five times.

Put the balloon in a warm place to dry. When the surface is hard, use the scissors to carefully cut the balloon in half.

Paint the balloon with ladybird colours. Use pipecleaners to make the legs, and attach them with glue or sticky tape.

Look in books to see if there are any different coloured ladybirds, and paint the other papier mâché shape in those colours.

Insect mobile

Make a mobile

Hang this colourful mobile near a window, or even outside, and watch the insects fly around the flower as the breeze blows.

ladybird

You will need
- Coloured card
- Pencil
- Scissors
- Paintbrush
- Paints
- Thin wire
- String
- Tracing paper
- Strong thread
- Apron

Draw a large flower shape on coloured card and cut around the edge. Paint the flower with colours that you like.

Ask an adult to help you make a circle of wire. Tie four long pieces of string to the wire and knot the ends so the mobile can hang.

3

Trace or copy the insects on these pages or draw your own on to card. Cut them out and paint them to look like insects.

4

Ask an adult to make small holes in your flower and insects so you can tie them to the wire circle. Your mobile is now ready to hang.

dragonfly

bee

shield bug

Glossary

Abdomen – the large part of an insect's body, containing its digestive system

Antenna – a long, thin structure on an insect's head for touching and smelling

Artificial – man-made

Bee-keeper – a person who looks after honeybee hives

Bug – an insect with sucking mouthparts

Camouflage – a shape, colour or pattern that helps an animal to hide

Compost – a mixture of rotting plants

Crop – a plant grown in large amounts to provide food or materials

Divided – split into sections

Earth – the planet on which we live

Firefly – a glowing, night-time beetle that is also called a lightning bug

Flexible – able to bend without breaking

Foe – an enemy

Fungus – a plant-like organism, such as a toadstool, that lives on another organism, either living or dead

Glow-worm – a female wingless beetle that glows in the dark

Harvesting – gathering and storing food

Honeycomb – a wax structure made by bees

Larva – a young insect that has hatched out of an egg

Mammal – a hairy animal that feeds its young on milk

Mate – to breed or reproduce

Migration – the long journey that some animals make to find food or a mate

Moulting – when an animal moults, it gets rid of its hair or skin

Mouthpart – a structure on an insect's head used for feeding

Muscle – a part of the body that produces movement

Nectar – a sweet liquid made by plants

Oxygen – a colourless gas needed by all animals in order to survive

Poisonous – describes something that can make you very ill or even kill you if you swallow it

Pollen – a yellow powder found in the male part of a flower

Predator – an animal that hunts and eats other animals

Preserved – protected, kept in its original state

Prey – an animal that is killed or eaten by another animal

Protein – a substance needed by living things for growth and repair

Pupa – a protective case around a developing adult insect

Queen – a female that lays the eggs in a group of social insects

Sap – a liquid found in the stems and trunks of plants

Skeleton – the structure that supports an animal's body

Social – living in a group with others of the same kind, or species

Sting – a sharp needle on an insect's body for injecting poison

Survival – staying alive

Termite – a soft-skinned, ant-like creature

Thorax – part of an insect's body between its head and abdomen

Thrive – to do well

Tropical – an area near the equator where it is hot all the year round

Veins – narrow tubes that carry blood

Parent and teacher notes

This book includes material that would be particularly useful in helping to teach children aged 7–11. It covers many elements of the English and Science curricula and provides opportunities for cross-curricular lessons, especially those involving Geography and Art.

Extension activities:

Writing
Each double-page information spread has a title, introduction and three paragraphs of text, each with its own sub-heading.

1) Choose any animal in this book and write a report on it, using this structure.

2) On page 37 a bird is shown eating an insect. Write about the incident in one of these styles:
- An article for a magazine called *Insect News.*
- A report about food chains.
- A diary entry by the bird.
- A flowchart or text showing the process from when the bird spotted the insect to how it was digested.

Speaking and listening
1) Make notes for a two-minute presentation comparing two insects in the book.

2) Act out a one-minute play describing a day in the life of an insect from its viewpoint.

Science
The topic of insects relates to the scientific themes of habitats, growth and health, food chains (and webs) and interdependence. This book offers links with the themes of life cycles (p28); food chains (p36); habitats (pp32 and 38); forces (p38 – how do these insects move on and in water?); gases (p18 – the uses of gases as poisons, and to make sounds and smells; p41 – the firefly uses oxygen) and materials (p33 – the wasps chew wood and mix it with their spit to build their paper nests).

Cross-curricular links
1) Art and literacy: Design your own insect and create a profile showing its habitat, diet and behaviour.

2) Art: Choose suitable materials to copy illustrations such as the large dragonfly on page 6. Paint a picture of an animal hiding itself with camouflage (page 16).

3) Geography: Investigate the long migration of the monarch butterfly. Track the journey from start to finish. Why do they make this journey?

Using the projects

Children can follow or adapt these projects at home. Here are some ideas for extending them:

Page 42: Mark out a square metre of long grass, flowers or fallen logs. Use a collecting jar and magnifying glass to study the insects that are in it. Create a field guide to your area.

Page 44: Instead of a balloon, create the shape using chicken wire. Or make an insect out of Modrock, a quick-drying plaster of paris material. Why stop with one type of insect? There are hundreds of different insects you can make. Use water balloons for the smaller models.

Page 46: Design and make an insect with some moving parts, such as a claw or jaws. Write creative 'life stories' about each of the insects on the mobile. Put them together to form a book. Read the stories aloud or act them out.

- Insects are more numerous than all other types of animal in the world put together.

- The noisiest insect in the world is the male cicada, which can be heard from 400 metres away.

- The house fly can be dangerous to humans because it carries so many diseases. It also reproduces at a very fast rate. A pair of flies have an astonishing 5,000 million young a year.

- A migrating monarch butterfly once travelled 3,432 kilometres from Canada to Mexico. The monarch is the fastest-flying butterfly, clocked at a top speed of 22 kilometres per hour.

- The human flea can jump 20 centimetres into the air. This is 60 times its body length and the same as a person jumping 110 metres!

- At 100 grams, the goliath beetle of equatorial Africa is the heaviest insect in the world. This is the same as a newborn kitten. The male can be over 11 centimetres long from the tips of its horns to the end of its abdomen.

- Ladybirds won't fly if the temperature is below 13° C.

- A ladybird's wings are so thin you can see right through them.

- Some insects can mimic other poisonous insects in order not to be hunted.

- Imagine being headless! A cockroach can live for an entire week... without its head! After being beheaded, the animal can survive for a long time, but there is one problem. Without a head, it has no mouth through which to drink water, so it eventually dies of thirst.

- Insects can see movements that take place in as little as 1/1000th of a second.

- Caterpillars have over 2,000 muscles in their tiny bodies.

- Some mosquitoes hunt by detecting their prey's body heat and homing in on it.

- Butterflies and moths are found in all places except Antarctica.

- Earwigs got their name from a myth that they crawl inside people's ears when they are sleeping! In truth, they never do.

- Leafcutter ants can lift and carry enormous weights. Some of their loads are equivalent to a young child carrying a 10-tonne truck!

- When bees discover a good source of nectar they tell other bees by doing a strange dance. But not all bees 'speak' the same language – bees from one area cannot understand bees from other areas.

- A shocking 2.5 million people die each year in Africa from the bite of the malaria-carrying mosquito. This makes mosquitoes the most dangerous creatures alive.

- An adult dragonfly can see nearly 360 degrees.

- Glow-worms are not actually worms; they are in fact beetles!

Insect quiz

The answers to these questions can all be found by looking back through the book. See how many you get right. You can check your answers on page 56.

1) How many legs does an insect have?
   A – Four
   B – Six
   C – Eight

2) Butterflies and moths have wings covered in tiny…
   A – Scales
   B – Spots
   C – Spikes

3) What do head lice eat?
   A – Blood
   B – Leaves
   C – Skin

4) Which insect is good at weightlifting?
   A – Leafhopper
   B – Rhinoceros beetle
   C – Ladybird

5) What makes an insect's wings so strong?
   A – Veins
   B – Muscles
   C – Bones

6) What noise do cockroaches make when they are disturbed?
   A – Clicking
   B – Squealing
   C – Hissing

7) How do flies eat their food?
   A – By chopping it up
   B – By rolling it into a ball
   C – By turning it into a soupy mush

8) Which insect feeds on damp wood?
   A – Death-watch beetle
   B – Grasshopper
   C – Ladybird

9) What is the third stage of many insects' lives?
   A – Egg
   B – Adult
   C – Pupa

10) Which insect young live underwater for their first year?
   A – Dung beetles
   B – Damselflies
   C – Earwigs

11) Honeybees make honey from…
   A – Flower nectar
   B – Water
   C – Mud

12) Which insect can walk on the surface of water?
   A – Pond skater
   B – Dragonfly
   C – Grasshopper

Books to read
Beastly Bugs by Lynn Huggins Cooper, Franklin Watts, 2008
Classifying Animals: Insects by Sarah Wilkes, Wayland, 2007
From Egg to Adult: The Life Cycle of Insects by Richard and Louise Spilsbury, Heinemann Library, 2004
How Does It Grow: Butterfly by Jinny Johnson, Franklin Watts, 2009
I Wonder Why Caterpillars Eat So Much by Belinda Weber, Kingfisher, 2006
Weird Bugs by Kathryn Smith, Kingfisher, 2010

Places to visit
Bug House at World Museum, Liverpool
www.liverpoolmuseums.org.uk
At the Bug House you can get closer than you ever imagined to a wide variety of insects. Watch the leafcutter ants in action and learn about how insects play an important role in making a wildlife-friendly environment in the garden.

Edinburgh Butterfly and Insect World
www.edinburgh-butterfly-world.co.uk
Visit the tropical rainforest and experience a tropical rainstorm first hand. You will also see the working honeybee hives and many more fascinating insects.

Stratford-Upon-Avon Butterfly Farm
www.butterflyfarm.co.uk
Whatever the weather you can take a stroll through the undercover rainforest, learn about a butterfly's life cycle and make a visit to Insect City. You will meet a wide range of interesting insects and even witness leafcutter ants marching above your head!

The Natural History Museum, London
www.nhm.ac.uk
Take a trip through the butterfly jungle, learn about their life cycle and habitats. Discover all sorts of insects in the creepy crawly gallery, even edible ones!

Websites
www.channel4learning.com
A useful website for children and teachers with a wide range of topics, including insects.

www.sciencemuseum.org.uk
A useful website for all aspects of science.

www.endangeredspecies.org
Learn about all the endangered insects in the world.

www.nhm.ac.uk
With a section just for children you will find a picture gallery, fun and games and facts about insects.

http://kids.nationalgeographic.com
Games, videos, stories, facts and activities on all science topics, including insects.

Insect quiz answers

1) B	7) C
2) A	8) A
3) A	9) C
4) B	10) B
5) A	11) A
6) C	12) A